Budgerig

Budgerigars as ι ∪ιₛ.

Budgerigar book for care, costs, feeding, health and training.

By

Darren Ludwig.

Table of Contents

Table of Contents 3

Introduction 4

Chapter 1. Meet the Budgerigar 6

Chapter 2. Varieties.. 10

Chapter 3. Buying a Budgerigar 18

Chapter 4. Training Your Budgerigars 29

Chapter 6. Caring For Your Budgerigar 35

Chapter 7. Budgerigar Nutrition 43

Chapter 8. Breeding Your Budgerigars... 56

Chapter 9. Budgerigar Health 63

Introduction

The budgerigar (*Melopsittacus undulatus*) is actually a small member of the parrot family, and one of the most popular pet birds in the world. Originally from Australia, in its native territory large flocks can commonly be seen constantly roving over the semi-arid plains. They migrate over the continent as the weather changes, spending the summer in southern regions, and the winter in the warmer north.

Budgerigars are beautiful creatures and one of the big reasons for that is their incredibly varied and vibrant plumage. Budgerigars come in a wide variety of different colors and patterns, each one as striking as the next and each able to tell us something about that bird. They are nomadic, moving to new areas in search food and water. This means they can be found in many parts of Australia, from the inland desert areas to some coastal regions.

Wild budgerigars live in flocks that can vary from a few birds to huge, noisy masses. When there is plenty of food the wild budgerigars will breed prolifically, producing three clutches of up to seven or eight chicks, although four is the average. However, the outback of Australia can go years without rain and reach temperatures of 49°C (120°F), burning up any food or water. In these times the budgerigars do not breed, and many die.

The budgerigar is a friendly bird with great powers of mimicry, and some individuals have the ability to use more than 500 words if given plenty of encouragement whilst still young. In fact, the best time to start training a budgerigar is from the age of 6 weeks when they are still very receptive to learning new words and sounds. By contrast, training an adult bird over 6 months of age is often unsuccessful.

Males and females can be easily distinguished by the color of their cere (the area above the beak encircling the nostrils). In adult males this is blue, whereas in adult females it is a pink-brown color, but this may be variable in certain colors and juvenile birds. They can live 10 - 15 years in captivity.

Chapter 1. Meet the Budgerigar

When it comes to pet birds, budgerigars have been popular options for years. These small parrots can be found in just about any pet store, but they're generally only found in the wild in Australia. Although it's not unusual to come across budgerigars of many different colors and patterns, those variations have come about through strategic, carefully planned breeding over the years. Despite their small size, these birds make fascinating pets. They have been charming people for years with their playful personalities, gorgeous coloring, intelligence and sociability. Budgerigars are affordable pets, and they are easy to care for as well.

With budgerigars, there's a lot more than meets the eye. Until you've actually taken the time to get to know a budgerigar, it's easy to assume that they are like any other bird. In the wild, budgerigars are prized for their bright, vibrant feathers. In captivity, they are popular for being easy, fun pets to have in the home. People have been breeding budgerigars for decades to develop exciting new color variations and markings. If you're thinking about adopting one, you can take your pick from more than 100 different variations.

A Brief History of the Budgerigar
Budgerigars have ancestors that stretch back for millennia. In fact, these birds first appeared on earth long before humans. They are native to Australia, and the first humans who came into contact with them were most likely the aborigines of that land. The first recorded

description of the budgerigar was made in 1805 by an English zoologist and botanist named George Shaw. The first budgerigar was brought to Europe by an English ornithologist named John Gould in 1840, and the first captive breeding began just a decade later during the 1850s. Although the first recorded color variation wasn't made until 1870, a wide variety of variations followed shortly thereafter. The budgerigar's popularity as a household pet rose dramatically during the 20th century, and the bird continues to be a very popular pet to this day.

Etymology
In some places, budgerigars are commonly referred to as "parakeets." That's misleading, however, because the term "parakeet" can refer to one of several dozen kinds of small parrots that have long feather trails. Other common names for the budgerigar include budgerigar, common pet parakeet, shell parakeet, canary parrot, flight bird, love bird, scallop parrot, zebra parrot and warbling grass parakeet. Variations on the word "budgerigar" include betcherrygah and budgerygah.

Even though budgerigars are typically called parakeets, especially in the United States, they are just one of over 100 species commonly referred to as parakeets, a widely diverse class of tiny, slender parrots spread out over more than a dozen genera in the subfamily Psittacinae of the family Psittacidae.

There's a lot of debate out there about the origins of the term "budgerigar." Many believe that it is derived from the Aboriginal word "betchegara," which means "good to eat." Others think that it comes from various Australian slang terms. For example, "budgery" means "good," and "gar" means "cockatoo." It is possible that the two terms were put together to create the name of the lovable pet parrot that is so popular today.

The budgerigar's scientific or binomial name is Melopsittacus undulatus. The term was coined by John Gould, the same English ornithologist that originally brought the first budgerigars to Europe. The first part, Melopsittacus, is Greek and means "melodious parrot," which is quite fitting. The second part, undulatus, is Latin and means "wave-patterned" or "undulated." That term clearly refers to the scalloped or undulated patterns that give the budgerigar such a distinct appearance.

Enrichment

Budgerigars are social animals, so it is a good idea to get two or more. They are more active and fun to watch when kept in groups. If your budgerigar has been hand-raised or you want them to talk, then it is fine to keep them alone as long as you provide the company they need to be happy.

Training budgerigars to talk is easy (but it all depends on the individual bird). Talk to your budgerigar in a soft manner at night, starting with simple 'ch' sounding words. During the day have your budgerigar near the TV or radio, as this can encourage social interaction. Your budgerigar is more likely to mimic a feminine voice, so keep this in mind. Both male and female budgerigars can be trained to talk, but males seem to learn faster.

Do budgerigars make good pets?

If you ask me, budgerigars make awesome pets! They are very active, playful birds, and they are incredibly intelligent. Some (but not all) budgerigars learn to talk, there are even budgerigars have a 100+ word vocabulary! Budgerigars can easily become finger tame while they are young with some diligent training, even if they were not hand-fed as babies. Many owners of fully tamed budgerigars will swear that their budgerigar thinks it's a human! Even if a budgerigar is not tamed, they still make enjoyable pets. Their antics and singing will brighten up any room in your home. And budgerigars that are not finger tame still can become friendly towards you, and even still learn to talk.

It's important to keep in mind that if you have (or plan to get) only one budgerigar, it's imperative that you socialize with him or her every day. Budgerigars, as with all parrots, are flock birds, and it is important to their mental health to have interaction with others. If you tame your budgerigar, you can provide him (or her) with the social interaction it needs by spending time with it every day (even if he or she just hangs out with you while you do your homework or clean up around the house). If you don't have the time or inclination to tame your budgerigar, then you must plan on getting at least two budgerigars so that they can provide each other the social interaction they need to be happy and healthy.

There are some downsides to keeping budgerigars as pets that you should be aware of. You should know that budgerigars can be messy. Seeds and feathers tend to scatter around the cage, so you'll have to sweep or vacuum often. A cage skirt (available at pet stores) can help cut down on the mess. You also have to be diligent enough to make sure your budgerigar always has fresh food and water, and to make sure the cage bottom gets cleaned about once a week. Budgerigars can also be a bit noisy, although they are not quite as noisy as most parrots. Budgerigars spend several hours a day, especially mornings and evenings, chirping and singing and sometimes squawking. This is normal behavior, and most people enjoy the singing and chatter of budgerigars. However, if the noise does not appeal to you or may bother other people that you live with, you may need to consider closely where you put the cage or if a budgerigar is the right pet for you. Covering the cage at night will keep your budgerigars quiet from bed time until you wake them up in the morning, but the rest of the day is fair game for budgerigar banter.

Chapter 2. Varieties

I am sure you have noticed that there is a huge array of budgerigar varieties and colors. We have covered the basic colors so I thought we had better look at the varieties.

If you know which variety you are interested in then check if they have their own page on the list below. However, if you are trying to learn more about the different varieties then read on. I have grouped the varieties differently than most people as I wanted it easy for beginners to get a handle on the many types, as they differ visually. They are grouped by how they look rather than how they are inherited.

Albino or Lutino Budgerigar
The Albino budgerigar variety (and the Lutino too) are created by the Ino gene, so are often just called Inos. The Ino gene removes all the melanin (the substance that creates all the dark colors in the feathers, skin and eyes). So a blue series budgerigar becomes white and all the green series ones become yellow. Albino is the term for a white Ino, and Lutino is the term for a yellow Ino.

Recognizing a Lutino or Albino Budgerigar
The Ino gene removes the dark shade from the skin and beak, leaving the bird with pink legs and an orange beak. It removes the blue shade from the cocks' cere (flesh around the nostrils) too so they have a flesh/skin colored cere whilst the hen is the usual rough brown shade, as this is not caused by melanin. The dark color of the eye is also gone, leaving a red eye with a white iris ring (sometimes no iris ring is present), and the cheek patches are silvery white.

Usually, only the white and yellow colors are left, so an Ino can hide the fact that it also has other varieties present. This is referred to as masking, so an Ino may be masking Spangle, or Dominant Pied, etc. You would not be able to see these varieties but they are present in the genes and could be passed on to offspring. The only varieties that should show are the Yellow Faces or Golden Faces on an Albino budgerigar, as seen below. These are sometimes called Creaminos and they look this way because the yellow color is not caused by melanin, so is not removed.

The only exception to the above rule is the Lacewing budgerigar, a composite of Cinnamon and Ino. In their case, the Cinnamon and Ino genes are present on the same chromosome and for some reason light brown markings and pale violet cheek patches are visible. This makes a lovely white or yellow bird with pale brown markings! The Lacewing is often spoken of as if it were a variety, but it is actually a composite (the same as a Spangle Opaline, or Cinnamon Recessive Pied for example) as it is made up of Ino and Cinnamon. The Ino and Cinnamon tend to be inherited together so it appeared to be a new variety at first, so was given its own name.

The other interesting thing that can happen is that sometimes a faint 'suffusion' of the body color can show in certain lights. The Ino budgerigar has a tiny bit of blue suffusion showing by its wing and under its tail. This is not an actual patch of blue body color. There is a lovely variety called the Texas Clearbody. This variety arose from a mutation in the Ino gene and so is related to Inos genetically, but will be discussed separately. The board includes Lacewings and Texas Clearbodys as they belong to the Ino group of varieties.

Blackface Budgerigar
This is a new variety that appeared in the 1990's in the Netherlands. Two blue birds with unusual markings were seen and bought by a breeder there. He bred them with his birds and managed to produce a small flock of them. Unfortunately, they were all kept together, rather than being spread between a few breeders, and an illness struck and killed them, so it is thought that the variety had been lost.

The Cinnamon Budgerigar

The throat spots, wing markings and barring on a Cinnamon budgerigar are a lovely warm brown shade. The color on the body is reduced to a paler shade than normal (maybe 2/3 as dark), and the feet and legs are pink rather than gray. The long tail feathers are the usual color but the quill is brownish. As chicks, cinnamons have dark, plum-colored eyes, but these darken as they grow until it is difficult to distinguish from a normal black eye. The cere is the same color as in wild type birds. This variety usually has a lovely soft look to their body feathers which combines with their markings to make them very attractive.

The Normal Budgerigar

The Normal budgerigar is one whose markings match with the wild type budgerigar. The budgerigar can be any of the basic body colors, but so long as it has the wild type markings it will be of the normal variety. So you can have Sky-blue Normal, Grey Normal, Dark Green Normal, etc.

Starting with a wild budgerigar, the body color is a lovely bright light green, with a yellow face. Along the bottom edge of the face are six small black spots and sitting over the outer of these on each side is a violet cheek patch. From the forehead, back and down to between the wings they have black and yellow stripes. The feathers on the wings are blackish with yellow edging, with the long flight feathers being black-blue with a thick yellow bar only visible when the wings are extended. The long tail feathers are a lovely dark teal blue, with the tail coverts having a thick yellow bar through them. The eyes have a black pupil surrounded by a white circle called the iris ring. The legs and feet are gray. A male budgerigar can be recognized by the smooth blue cere, while the female has a brown, usually rough cere.

The normal budgerigar can come in all the basic body colors: Light Green, Dark Green, Olive, Grey Green, Violet Green, Sky-blue,

Cobalt, Mauve, Gray and Violet. It can also be combined with other varieties that alter the color of the markings to produce many beautiful birds: Cinnamon, Graywing, Clearwing, Dilute, Fallow, Yellow Face to name a few. Basically, any bird that still has the wild type markings is normal, so you can have a normal Cinnamon or a normal Yellow Face Blue, etc. It is usual just to skip using the term normal and refer to them simply as a Cinnamon or a Yellow Faced Blue for convenience.

Opaline Budgerigar
The opaline budgerigar is a particularly common variety and is often combined with others to create some very lovely birds. However, it is sometimes tricky to get a look at a pure one to see how they look without other varieties present.

The Opaline budgerigar has the barring over its head and down between its shoulders greatly reduced. The markings on the back between the wings should be gone, though often they are present but finer and sparse (and in some show types the markings have become very heavy). The opaline gene also softens the body color slightly so that it is a little paler than a normal of the same color. The main feature is also that the body color of the budgerigar (i.e. green, blue, gray etc.) has replaced the yellow or white on the wings. So instead of having black markings on a yellow or white background, they are on a green or blue or gray background. The body color also often shows on the black part of the wing feather. This is called opalescence and can be attractive.

Another defining feature is the enlargement of a stripe of white or yellow on the flight feathers. Normal budgerigars have a stripe along the flights but it is thinner than on an opaline and does not reach all the way across the feathers towards the edge of the wing. This means that when the wing is folded, when perched, you may see a small bit of it but often none at all.

In opaline budgerigars, this strip is wider and extends across the feathers fully so when the bird is perched you can see a section of white or yellow on the flights. Apart from these features the eyes, feet and legs, and cere color are all the same as normal. The long tail feathers often have body color or white running down them as well as the normal color.

The Beautiful Spangle Budgerigars
The spangle budgerigar is one of the favorites. They can look quite stunning, but often the markings are faded and partially missing, which is sad. The spangle comes in two forms: the single factor and the double factor spangle. The single factor has just one spangle gene, whilst the double factor has two. For now, let's discuss the physical appearance of each.

The single factor spangle has the markings on the wings, the throat spots and the tail feathers altered. The wing feathers appear to have a black edge with either a yellow or white center and are often described as having the normal markings reversed. I do not like this description as it is clear when looking at a spangle budgerigar that the feathers still have the white or yellow edge, then a thin black pencil line, then the center of the feather is yellow or white.

The throat spots are often all or partly missing but if present look like targets, with a yellow or white center. The long tail feathers can be like the wing feathers with a thin line near the edge, or they may be plain white or yellow.

The double factor spangle is a pure white or yellow bird, though sometimes with a slight suffusion of body color. Both types of spangle have normal dark eyes with a white iris ring and normal colored ceres. Their feet and legs can be gray or fleshy pink, single factor spangles can have either violet or silvery white cheek patches (or a mixture of both) and the double factor has silver cheek patches.

Spangle can combine with any other variety to create many lovely mixes. Spangle opalines are common and can vary a lot in their appearance. The markings are reduced over the head and shoulders, and the body color is present on the wings. The Spangle opaline has lost some of its markings and has a lot of cobalt on the wings. It is not uncommon for the markings on a spangle opaline to be body colored rather than black. It has heavier than usual markings for a spangle and less body color on the wings.

What is a budgerigar variety?

Sometimes a mutation occurs that alters the color or pattern of a budgerigar's markings. If this is able to be passed on to chicks it can become a new variety. A variety is separate from a budgerigar's base color. They can occur on any color and are basically overlaid, so you would describe your budgerigar by its color and its variety. For example, a wild budgerigar would be a light green (the color) normal (the variety), or you may have a sky-blue (the color) opaline (the variety).

I have thought long and hard about organizing the varieties in a way that makes it easy to find the one you want if you don't know what it is called. This has turned out to be a bit tricky, and will probably not suit everyone! I have grouped them in the way that they differ from the normal budgerigar. So we had better start with that...

Normal is the term for budgerigars whose markings match with the wild type. The budgerigar can be any of the basic body colors, but so long as it has the wild type markings it will be of the normal variety.

There are several varieties which have markings that are not black.

Brown markings:
• Cinnamon
• Fallow
• Lacewing

• Brown-wing

Grey to very pale or non-existent markings:
• Gray-wing
• Dilute
• Clearwing
• Faded.

(Texas Cearbodies have gray primaries but the majority of their markings are black so I have included them in the 'None of the above' category below).

Varieties with the pattern of its markings different than a normal:
There are a few varieties which have marking patterns that are different from the normal:
• Blackface
• Opaline
• Spangle.

Varieties that have pied markings:
There are several types of pieds:
• Dominant Pied - also known as Australian or Banded Pied
• Recessive Pied - also known as Danish Pied
• Clearflight - also known as Dutch Pied
• Mottled - not an actual pied, but looks like one.

Varieties with no markings at all:
These varieties have the markings and all or most of the body color, removed:
• Inos – albino and lutino
• Double factor spangle
• Dark eyed clears.

None of the above?

If none of the above matches what you are looking for, try these:

• Yellow Face/Golden Face
• Clear-body
• Crested
• Anthracite
• Saddleback
• Dark-wing.

Composites

Finally, bear in mind that many budgerigars are a mix of more than one variety; a composite. There are so many combinations I couldn't list them all.

So if you are trying to work out what varieties your budgerigar is I would suggest starting with marking color, and then work through the other categories, adding any other varieties that fit. It may not be the most accurate method but it should give you somewhere to start from. There is a particularly lovely composite called Rainbow. It is a blue bird with Opaline, Clearwing and Yellow Face all present.

Chapter 3. Buying a Budgerigar

Choosing A Good Budgerigar

These days apples aren't apples, meaning they are not all the same, and similarly, budgerigars just aren't budgerigars... there are many varieties of budgerigars in terms of vitality, stamina, color, feather, body structure and mentality. Depending on your purpose and intent for choosing and buying your budgerigars, these differences can become very, very important, especially if you are choosing and buying your budgerigars to be pets.

Beauty is in the eye of the beholder, yet personality attributes, stamina and fitness, vitality, susceptibility to disease, long life expectancy, the ability to fly well or lack of these are real. Many modern exhibition budgerigars and their discarded not-up-to standard off-spring are deficient in one or more of the above qualities. I hope that many budgerigar breeders of the future will re-evaluate the criteria they use for selecting budgerigars to produce future generations for the pet market. In the meantime, "buyers beware"!

The Cost of Purchasing a Budgerigar

How much will it cost to buy the bird you want? It depends on the species, and whether you buy from a professional breeder or another source such as a pet store. Beyond the cost of the budgerigar itself, new owners should budget for things like pellets and other dietary needs like seeds and fruits, properly-sized cages and even bird-proofed rooms for larger birds to fly around.

Depending on the breeder, availability and your location, the cost of your budgerigar may fluctuate outside the given ranges. In general (depending on the breed), housing, feeding, and caring for a bird is less expensive than caring for a dog or cat, but the costs can rise dramatically depending upon the lifespan of the bird and healthcare needs.

- First-year cost: $295/£217.83
- Annual cost: $185/£136.6 (plus unforeseen vet costs)
- Total lifetime cost (avg. lifespan of parakeet: 10-15 years): $3,500/£2584.4.

Other first-year costs:
- Cage ($70/£51.69)
- Purchase price, which ranges from $12/8.86 to $65/48 for a budgerigar.

After the first year, annual costs include:
- Food ($75/£55.38)
- Toys and treats ($25/£18.46)
- Routine vet check-ups ($85/£62.76).

Lifespan varies depending on the species, but budgerigars tend to live between 10 and 15 years if given proper veterinary care.

Budgerigars are relatively inexpensive to care for and feed, but a diet consisting only of seeds is not enough; veterinarians recommend a diet that includes pellets, fresh fruits, and vegetables including leafy greens. Because they live so long, you really need to make sure you are buying the right bird for you and your family. In order to find a good budgerigar, you need to assess the bird's health, personality, and happiness before purchase. Finding a budgerigar that will be a long-term happy member of your family takes some diligence on your part, as well as a willingness to walk away from a bird that's just not right for you.

Choosing a Healthy Budgerigar

Locate budgerigars for sale from a reputable seller
You can find budgerigars for sale online, in want-ads, or in pet stores. You can also get one from your local animal shelter.

Wherever you get your budgerigar from, make sure the seller has healthy and humanely-treated birds.

Look at online reviews for the sellers you find. Are most buyers satisfied with the birds that they purchased from the seller? If you have a friend that has budgerigars, ask them where you can get good birds. This is especially helpful if they got their bird, or birds, recently.

Visit a store or an individual seller
Assess how they make you feel. Does the space feel clean and well cared for? Do you think the people working at the store or the person selling the birds feels responsible and invested in the health and happiness of the birds? If any of this feels wrong, walk away.

Ask the seller how they care for their birds
Make sure they are cleaning the birds' cages regularly. Are the sellers cleaning their hands before handling the birds? These are simple but important things that keep budgerigars healthy and happy.

Examine the cage the budgerigars are in
Budgerigars need a clean and spacious cage. Are there so many budgerigars in there they can't all move? Is the cage or bin dirty? Does the condition of the cage line up with what the seller told you they do to care for their birds? Do the birds have water? Do the birds have appropriate food, such as seeds, pellets, and vegetables? These are all important things to assess before moving forward with purchasing a budgerigar.

Consider whether the birds look healthy and happy
Are the birds interacting with one another? Look at the head, body, and legs of each bird you are considering. If it is healthy and happy its feathers should be smooth and shiny, not all puffed up. It should have a healthy appetite, so you should see it eating. Its beak and feet should not be crusted. Its vents should be clear and it should not

have any nasal discharge. The feathers should have an appearance that is shiny, sleek, and smooth. The budgerigars should not have any growths or abnormalities. The budgerigars' feet should be clear of mites and its toes should be clean and smooth.

Choosing a Budgerigar based on Personality and Appearance

Assess your potential budgerigar's temperament

If it is healthy and happy then it should be active and seem happy. Does it move around, eat, and drink water? While a budgerigar should be relatively calm when left alone, it is natural for a budgerigar to tighten its feathers when you come near its cage, so don't read that behavior negatively. Usually, the budgerigars from pet shops are not hand-tamed, which means that you will have to be willing to take the time to help it get accustomed to your hand, if you want to be able to hold it. If you want to buy a budgerigar that is already hand-tamed, you will need to go to a specialized budgerigar breeder.

Look for a budgerigar that is young

You can tell the age of a budgerigar by the black bars on the forehead. A young budgerigar (under 4 months) will have black bars all the way down to the cere, which is the fleshy part above the beak. Above 4 months, the bars will disappear. If the budgerigar is molting it is around 6 months old; this is a good age to train a budgerigar.

Determine if your potential budgerigar is male or female

This only matters if you have a preference and only works when they are old enough that the bars are gone. For males, the cere is blue. For females, the cere will be very light blue, beige, or brown. Male budgerigars are slightly better talkers, so if you are concerned with that you might want to make sure you get a male bird. However, a young, healthy bird of either sex can be a great talker with the right training.

Pick a bird that is attractively colored

If you are purchasing a budgerigar from a seller that has a lot of healthy and active birds, then feel free to pick your budgerigar based on looks. Budgerigars come in a huge variety of colors, so pick the color combination that you like best.

Buying Budgerigars ? Some more factors you need to consider!

Is your family ready for a new pet? Perhaps a budgerigar could be right for you! Like all pets, budgerigars have their pros and cons. While these feathered companions can be charming, silly and entertaining, they also require a lot of care, can make a big mess and might drive you a bit crazy with their squawking. Not sure if a bird would be a good addition to your home? Here are things to consider before buying a bird

Attention

These intelligent animals thrive in stimulating environments where they spend time with humans or other birds. In fact, a budgerigar may be driven to engage in destructive behaviors, like plucking, if he is isolated or does not get enough attention. When you're deciding if a budgerigar is right for your family, you should consider the amount of attention you can devote to this pet. If no one is home all day, a bird might not be the best pet for your family.

Time

After spending quality time interacting with a budgerigar, you, or your child, will also need to prepare his food, clean his cage, clean his food bowls and help him with his grooming (please note that we will use 'he' for ease and that females are also available). It's also important for a budgerigar to have supervised time outside of his cage. Be prepared to take on these responsibilities if your family opts for a feathered friend.

Commitment

Many budgerigars live a long life. As such, adding a bird to your family has the potential to be a lifelong commitment. Even smaller budgerigar can live for 18 years, so if you're thinking of getting a budgerigar as a pet for your child, they may not be around to care for their pet during future summers or college years.

Safety

Unfortunately, some budgerigars tend to bite, especially if they bond with a particular person and feel jealous or needy. While this is certainly not always the case, it's important to consider the possible safety issues that come along with having this type of pet.

Other Pets

If you have other pets in the house, you can still have a budgerigar! You should, however, consider several factors before making that leap. The cartoons are right; sometimes birds and cats just don't get along, so you'll have to start out with supervised interactions.

Space

A budgerigar will need an appropriately sized cage - the larger, the better. Some cages are as big as five feet wide. Make sure that you have the necessary space for a cage, stand and other supplies.

Noise

Do you love peace and quiet? Then buying a budgerigar might not be the best choice for you. Even small budgerigars tend to make an awful lot of noise, and that noise isn't always pleasant.

Veterinarian

Not all vets will treat birds, so before bringing a bird home, check that you have a local avian veterinarian available to you.

Expense

As with any pet, it's important that you keep your budget in mind. Bird food, toys, vet bills, grooming costs, cages and stands can add up rather quickly.

Breeders and Rescues

Unfortunately, some birds are illegally taken from their wild homes and sold on the pet market. As such, it's very important that you do some research and use a reputable breeder or rescue organization. Both will help you find the right bird for your family and provide any support that you need during the process.

Other factors to consider before meeting a breeder

- Consider joining an avicultural society.
- Get to know some aviculturists.
- Learn who is breeding birds successfully.
- Find out if they are buying birds frequently, as well as selling them. If they are buying birds frequently, the risk of you buying a bird incubating disease is likely to be increased.
- Ascertain which aviculturists breed the birds you want to buy.
- Establish the bona fides of the people you may deal with.
- Can you inspect their aviaries? Pay particular attention to the health of the birds, the food storage and preparation areas, cleanliness, the presence of vermin (rats, mice, cockroaches) and the space allowed per bird. Room to fly helps build stamina.
- Do they have a separate quarantine area?
- If there are any sick birds, postpone your purchases.
- If the aviaries are filthy, go elsewhere.
- If possible, get all your birds from the one breeder to minimize the risks of disease.

- Find out the "going rate" or expected price for the type of birds you want. This can usually be ascertained through the appropriate avicultural society.
- Beware of bargains! Often budgerigars being sold for bargain prices are found to have something wrong with them, to be infertile, or perhaps they have been illegally obtained. Old finches with only a year or so to live are sometimes sold to the unsuspecting.
- Remember to pair your budgerigars: give each a mate!

Buying budgerigars from a pet shop or bird dealer

If you intend to buy your birds from a pet shop or bird dealer, realize that the inherent risks of getting buying budgerigars incubating disease are greater because of many factors, such as:

- Budgerigars are usually sold from overcrowded small cages.
- Budgerigars are usually being bought and traded from many different sources, the disease-status of which is usually unknown.
- Budgerigars from different sources are often put in the same cage, or share the same air space. If one source is infected, the infection is likely to appear in the others after the appropriate incubation period, which means the budgerigars may appear well at the time of purchase but become ill in the first 6 weeks or so at home.
- Customers (strangers) get very close to the birds and often frighten or stress them.
- Customers are often already bird keepers and may carry "germs" on their hands and clothing. Some will be out shopping to replace a bird that has just died.

When intending to buy birds through a dealer or shop

- Check if cages are stacked one on another with birds below being defecated upon.

- Is the shop dusty? Remember Chlamydia, avian Circovirus (Psittacine Beak and Feather Disease Virus) and other agents and other germs can be spread in the dust.
- Try to see "out the back".
- Ask if you can organize to buy the birds through the dealer without them being put into the shop environment.
- Can you have them delivered or can you pick them up immediately?
- Arrange to buy the birds conditional to a satisfactory veterinary health check performed within 72 hours of purchase.

How to Buy A Budgerigar From Breeders

Below are some points to note before buying a budgerigar from budgerigar breeders:

Age

In most of the bird species, age is not an issue when buying, but to the budgerigar, you need to buy an immature one so that it doesn't escape from your home. When you buy a mature budgerigar, it will look for ways and means to escape to its home.

Size

Make sure not to buy a very small size of a budgerigar even if it is of the maturity age. This means there is a problem with its growth and might end up losing its life at that early age. It could also mean that it is suffering from a certain disease and in this case end up spreading to the other breed. Good budgerigar breeders will always advise you on that so as to be aware.

Sex

When buying your budgerigar, make sure to consider sex for the breeding purposes. All that you need to do is make sure that you have a balance of the male not to outweigh the female. With two males and maybe four or five females, you are likely to have few more budgerigars with time.

Health
There are many chances of losing a sick budgerigar. You can decide to buy the sick parakeet because it would be relatively cheaper but then again. However, other than losing the breed, you are likely to incur so many costs as you take care of its health by buying medicine and getting the best vets.

Contrary to other bird breeders, breeders will have a hard time and therefore may end up selling them at a quite higher price than expected. Make sure to go the most known budgerigar breeders for the best breeds and affordable ones as well. Before buying the budgerigars, you are supposed to have your cage ready at home waiting and some feed as well so that your new home is fully equipped.

Pet insurance
Budgerigars can live upwards of fifty years, and a lot can happen in that time. Accidents and injuries can occur, and as with humans, illness can take hold.

In addition to helping with vet fees, pet insurance can also cover you in case your budgerigar is stolen or dies. Pet insurance will also cover your budgerigar for proven loss resulting from fire, wind, storm, lightening or flood. Bird housing and enclosures can also be covered by budgerigar pet insurance policies.

How much is budgerigar insurance?
A basic policy for a budgerigar that is worth $405.45/£300 starts from around $58.49/£43.28 a year. Prices depend on the value of your pet, and the policy type you choose.

As with with many types of insurance, the cost may also vary according to different factors about you and your budgerigar.

A quote request for a budgerigar worth $405.45/£300 produced the following premiums:

- For vet fee cover up to $6757.5/£5,000 a sample quote came to around $25.68/£19 per month spread over 10 months. This cover also includes death cover, theft cover and weather perils.
- For vet fee cover up to $3378.75/£2,500 a sample quote came to around $21.62/£16 per month spread over 10 months. This cover also includes death cover, theft cover and weather perils.

Pet insurance also offers a policy which only covers death, theft and weather perils and excludes vet fees. A sample quote for this came to around $5.41/£4 per month spread over 10 months.

Pet insurance policies run for a 12 month period, so monthly renewal is not required.

Pet insurance does not differentiate between different types of budgerigar breeds, only providing the options of "a small bird" or "an exotic bird/bird of prey" (with budgerigars always falling under the exotic bird category). This may be good news for owners of birds who are more expensive to insure.

It is important to note that these are just examples and prices vary. Additionally, it is always important to consider what policy changes could occur at renewal, and to read the Policy Terms and Conditions in full to make sure you know what is and isn't covered by your policy.

Chapter 4. Training Your Budgerigars

A budgerigar is a lively and chatty little bird. If you've decided to buy one of these fantastic animals and have already read how to take care of a budgerigar, it's time to learn how to train it. Be prepared for a lot of fun!

Earning Your Budgerigar's Trust

Make your budgerigar feel at home
If your budgerigar is new, it will need time to get used to its cage. You should let it adjust for at least a few days and make sure that the bird is in a quiet environment before attempting to train it By this time, the budgerigar should start to relax and feel comfortable.

- Stay close to the cage. Talk to it quietly as you wait for it to adjust but do not try to handle it. It will get used to you in the course of a few days or weeks.
- Avoid loud noises and screams. Your budgerigar is likely to be stressed by this new environment.
- Name your budgerigar. Say it often, especially when you feed it, so that it gets used to its new name.
- Read your bird a story. This might sound strange but budgerigars like to hear their owner's voice. Reading them a book will sooth them and make your voice familiar.

Feed and water the budgerigar daily
The budgerigar will slowly recognize you as the one providing food. The bird will trust you faster and will be excited when seeing you.
Water and food should be changed daily, even if the budgerigar hasn't touched it. A new budgerigar will often refuse to eat for up to a week as it gets used to its new life.

Introduce your budgerigar to treats before training starts. Give it a piece of fruit or a few seeds. Your bird will love it and will be more willing to learn if it has an incentive. Don't go over the top with treats, as you want to keep your bird healthy.

Let the budgerigar fly in a room

Once the bird is at ease with you, you can let it fly in a room with all of the windows and doors closed. This extra space will make your budgerigar happy and will keep it fit for the forthcoming training.

To call it back, switch off all the lights and leave the curtain of one window open, but remember to close the window. The budgerigar will be attracted towards the light. Hold it gently and put it back inside the cage. Make sure that there is no cat or predator in the room. If you have a child, don't let him/her frighten the bird. Budgerigars are easily traumatized.

Teaching Tricks

Encourage physical contact

Once your budgerigar is settled, place your hand in the cage and keep it immobile. Repeat this for days to let your bird get used to your physical presence in the cage.

- When the budgerigar seems okay with your hand, place your finger inside the cage. Then push it slightly against your budgerigar's chest. This will encourage it to climb on your finger. Be patient, as the bird might be reluctant at first.
- If the bird is intimidated, just stroke its breast with the back of your finger. Show love and care.
- Alternatively, you can put a few seeds on your finger. Your budgerigar will probably climb on your hand to eat them. Doing this for a few days will teach your pet to trust you.

Start using directions

When talking to your budgerigar, start using instructions like "Up!" and "Down"" to coincide with its hopping on and off your finger. Repetition is the key to getting him to perform an action according to your words (which are just sounds to him).

- Offer a treat when your budgerigar does something following your instruction. This will reinforce the desired behavior.
- Be persistent and consistent. You will need to focus on one instruction at a time, and for quite a while until your budgerigar repeats on cue. Persevere and don't vary the routine; this increases the chances that your budgerigar will learn faster.

Teach your budgerigar to fly to you

Have your finger super-close, but not too close that your bird can just step up. It needs to hop. Bring your finger half an inch further and reward your budgerigar with millet each time your budgerigar flies to you. Practice this and bring your finger further and further each day.

You can also teach your budgerigar to fly to its perch. Point to the perch and say "go back to your perch". Reward the budgerigar when they go to the perch. If your bird seems clueless, set it down there and say "perch" and reward, but you must start when you're half an inch away.

Train your budgerigar to balance on a tennis ball

Once your bird knows basic directions, it's time to make things more difficult. Introduce a tennis ball in its cage and let the birds play for a few days. Follow the following steps:

- Try to put the budgerigar on top of the tennis ball and hold its body while the feet look for balance. Every time the budgerigar tries to balance itself with its feet, offer a treat.

- Don't force your bird to learn a trick for too long. 10-15 minutes per day is enough. Remember that your bird should have fun!
- Leave the ball in the cage. Your budgerigar will eventually understand the purpose of the exercise and balance on its own on the ball.
- Be gentle when you hold the budgerigar on the tennis ball. Remember that they are fragile birds.

Teach the budgerigar to climb a ladder

You can find plastic bird ladders in most pet shops. Fix it to the side of the cage. Your budgerigar will be naturally intrigued by the ladder and will want to climb it.

- Every time the bird tries to climb the ladder, say the same word, like 'climb', to let your bird make the association between its action and your order.
- The trick is to make your budgerigar climb when you order it. Be patient and gentle. Place your bird on the lowest end of the ladder and hold it. Say the word associated with climbing and release your budgerigar.
- Once your bird understands what is expected, don't place it on the lowest end of the ladder but a few centimeters from it. Increase the distance every day until your budgerigar obeys without physical contact.

Learning to speak and sing

Teach your budgerigar its name

It is easier to start with the animal's name, as it hears it all the time. Repeat your budgerigar's name every time you see it and when you bring food. Try to speak in a high-pitched voice and say the name slowly and clearly.

- Wait until the budgerigar is old enough. The bird should be at least three months old before it can speak.
- If you have more than one budgerigar, stick to the teaching of one name. You don't want to make it too hard at first.
- Don't forget to reward your budgerigar. If it doesn't learn quickly, don't punish it. It doesn't understand right or wrong and will just mistrust you.

Expand its vocabulary

Talented budgerigars can learn over a thousand words over their lifetime. Once your bird knows its name, target the words you want to teach. Your budgerigar will eventually make the connection between the words and the objects or actions.

- When you enter the room, systematically say 'hi coco [or the budgerigar's name]'. When you feed it, point at the seeds and say 'food'.
- Look at their body language and take advantage. When the bird is in a threatening posture (biting or pecking), say 'Angry'. When the budgerigar is resting on one leg and looking happy, say 'happy'.
- Your budgerigar can also say simple sentences. When your bird eats, say 'coco [or the bird's name] eats'. When it drinks, say 'coco drinks'.
- Don't teach your bird insults. The budgerigar will remember it for a long time and might embarrass you in front of your guests.

Teach your budgerigar a song

There is nothing funnier than having your bird sing a song. Your budgerigar can remember simple tunes and will happily delight the whole family. The easiest way to teach a song is to sing it over and over to your bird. Don't try to teach the whole song but just a few seconds.

- Pick a song you like. Remember that your budgerigar might sing it for a long time.
- Record yourself singing a song and play it to your bird when you're away. This is an extremely efficient way to teach a song without having to sing it a thousand times. You can do the same to teach words.
- The actual recording of a song might not be the best way to teach the bird. The instruments will probably disturb it.

Chapter 6. Caring For Your Budgerigar

The key to a happy and fulfilling life with your pet budgerigar is adequate care to maintain its well-being. Here are a few tips.

Handling your budgerigar

Budgerigars are tamed very well, although patience is required and it is important that they are handled from an early age. First of all, get the budgerigar used to being stroked while inside the cage, using a blunt stick or a spare perch to avoid being pecked! Stroke your budgerigar a couple of times each day and encourage him to climb or jump onto the perch or stick.

Once your budgerigar is happy with this, try using your hand instead of the stick. Be aware that it may take several weeks to get to this stage with your budgerigar.

To pick up a budgerigar, use your palm to cover its wings and back and gently hold your bird at the neck between your index and middle fingers. Move slowly, and avoid stressing the bird. Budgerigars will bite if stressed! Always pick up your budgerigar from a perch or while standing; never attempt to catch him while in flight.

A list of things you will need for your budgerigar

- **Cage** - Assuming you are planning on keeping your budgerigar indoors, you should get the largest cage you can afford in terms of money and space. Bars should be no wider than 12mm apart in order to prevent any unexpected breaks for freedom and should have some horizontal bars installed to facilitate climbing.
- **Cage cover** - To be used at night so that your budgerigar won't wake you up in the wee hours twittering away.

- **Water bowl** - Make sure your budgerigar has access to fresh water at all times, and clean his water bowl out regularly.
- **Seed bowl** - Take care not to overfill the seed bowl, as leftover seed can become damp and moldy. Throw out and replace any uneaten seed regularly, and always store your budgerigar's food in a dry, airtight container.
- **Grit** - A fine sprinkling of grit on the floor of the cage for your budgerigar to scrape and peck provides an important digestive aid.
- **Perch** - Various bars and perches within the cage are important in order to allow your budgerigar to roost.
- **Floor Lining** - Cover the floor of the cage with a newspaper in order to facilitate easy clean ups, and to provide a suitable surface for your budgerigar to walk on. Some people cover the floor of the cage with sand or sand sheets, but if a grit bowl is provided, this is not necessary.
- **Cuttlefish or a mineral block** - An important source of calcium and nutrients for your budgerigar. Provide at least one of the two.
- **Millet** - Budgerigars love eating sprays of millet, and have almost as much fun shredding the casings as they do eating it. Millet is only suitable as a treat or supplement, and not as your budgerigar's staple diet.
- **Tonic seed** - A vitamin and mineral enriched seed mixture to feed as a supplement to your budgerigar's everyday feed.
- **Toys** - Bells, toys and mirrors keep your budgerigar entertained on a day to day basis.

How to keep your budgerigar happy and healthy

Budgerigars can be kept alone if sufficient stimulation is provided, but are generally happier with other birds. In large aviaries, you can also mix budgerigars with other small parakeets.

Clean the cage and any equipment used in it regularly in order to make sure your budgerigar stays happy and healthy.

Your budgerigar will need a daily bath. This can either be provided in the form of a bowl of water on the floor of the cage or attached to the bars or alternatively some birds like being lightly sprayed with tepid water in order to groom themselves. Never use aerosol sprays around your budgerigar, and be aware of the cage's location in relation to other fumes they may become exposed to.

Always make sure the room your budgerigar is in is secure and contained when you let them out of the cage.

Budgerigars need their claws clipped several times a year. Talk to your vet about having this done- do not attempt to clip your budgerigar's claws yourself as a novice keeper.

Housing
The main thing to remember when buying a bird cage is that the bigger, the better! Even the smallest birds need plenty of room otherwise they will become very miserable, so make sure there's enough room for your bird to fly around between perches. A wire bird cage with a removable tray will make a wonderful home for your new budgerigar. Don't leave your budgerigar outside of their cage unless you're in the room.

Budgerigars love to fly, so the taller and bigger your cage is, the happier your budgerigar will be. It is best to remove the wire bottom above the cage's tray. This can trap small feet and can be very difficult to clean.

When Keeping Budgerigars, here is a rule of thumb: Everything in 3s!
- 3 Wing lengths: A good cage should be three times the budgerigar's wingspan. The cage should be at least 50 centimeters (19.7 in) D x 60 centimeters (23.6 in) H x 80 centimeters (31.5 in) W.

- 3 Bowls: Most cages have two. One bowl for food and another for water, an extra bowl is good for treats!
- 3 Toys: Budgerigars do get bored quickly, so have a number of different toys for them. Avoid mirrors, particularly with hand-raised budgerigars and those kept in groups.
- 3 Perches: Have perches of different widths, as this will exercise the budgerigar's feet. Natural perches are beneficial, as they are generally more comfortable and allow for further exercise than generic pine perches.

Budgerigars naturally live in large flocks so will be happiest in a spacious aviary set up. This should be an outdoor enclosure made of strong wire mesh (which should be zinc free), with an easily cleanable floor and plenty of room for the birds to fly around. In addition to the flying area, a sheltered sleeping area should be provided to protect from the worst of the harsh weather. There should also be the facility to provide supplementary heating in the winter. The shelter should also provide shade on sunny days. Perches can be placed at varying heights around the enclosure with branches of different diameters providing the most natural set up. It is also particularly important to ensure that the enclosure is secure, both to stop the birds getting out (double security doors are the best way to prevent an escape) and to stop predators getting in.

Alternatively, if an aviary is not an option or if you wish to tame the birds, then they may be housed indoors in a cage set up. Ideally, the cage should only be used for housing the bird at night or when unsupervised. A cage set up should also be as large as possible and must allow the bird to stretch its wings in all directions. The cage should be made of non-toxic material and be zinc free. It should be placed out of direct sunlight and draughts and situated away from any item that may give off toxic fumes. Certain household products such as tobacco smoke, Teflon from non-stick frying pans, plug-ins and deodorants can lead to irritation of the bird's respiratory tract and in some cases can be fatal.

We recommend changing the perches that are supplied with most cages (usually wooden dowel or plastic) to natural tree branches. Fruit trees are preferred and these should be washed thoroughly with an appropriate disinfectant before use. Natural tree branches prevent all of the common foot injuries that we see and prevent nail overgrowth. Sandpaper perch covers should not be used, as they simply abrade the feet and do not keep the nails short. In most budgerigars, the problem is sharp nails as opposed to long nails and at the bird's health check-up we can burr the nails and blunt them.

Ultraviolet lighting is important for birds, required both for natural behavior and calcium metabolism. Specific bird lamps are available and have recognized health benefits.

Different toys should be added and changed regularly to entertain birds. It is however important to bear in mind that many pet shop toys can be easily destroyed, so only sturdy toys should be used. When purchasing toys or cages always make sure that they are "zinc-free", as zinc poisoning is increasingly seen in captive birds. Be careful, as some fixings can contain zinc but yet the toy is zinc free. Household items such as keys, old paintwork, and lead weights can contain heavy metals and are potential sources of toxicity.

Free flight is an essential requirement and birds should be given the opportunity for exercise daily. It is however important to ensure that the room they are allowed to fly around in is totally secure with all windows, doors and chimneys blocked off, heaters and fans turned off and any potentially poisonous house plants removed.

Physical hazards around the home
Don't let your budgerigar fly free in an area or room of the house until you've established that it is bird safe. Be sure that there are no fans running, and that the blinds or curtains are at least partly-drawn on the windows. In addition, if there are large mirrors in the room, you should place stickers or ribbons on them. Budgerigars can

accidentally fly into windows and mirrors and injure themselves badly. Once your budgerigar learns the layout of your home, you may be able to remove the mirror decorations and have the blinds or curtains open. You'll also need to make sure that there is nothing your budgerigar could land on that might fall, such as trophies or decorations up on shelves. Reduce the amount of exposed electrical and computer cords to the bare minimum, and always keep your budgerigar away from these. Remove any plants unless you know they are safe for birds. For resources on safe or toxic plants and other items. Examine the area or room from a bird's point of view and try to identify and remove anything that might be a hazard. Even if you're sure a room is bird safe, you should never leave your budgerigar out of its cage unattended. You never know what kind of trouble he or she might get into, such as nibbling a stray cord, chewing your favorite book, falling behind furniture, or getting hurt accidentally.

Grooming
Budgerigars do not need a lot of grooming and a healthy budgerigar will groom itself regularly. If your budgerigar appears un-groomed, this is usually a sign of illness and they may need some vitamin or medication supplements.

Clipping wings is a potentially dangerous process so it is best to visit the vet if you wish to do so. Only ever clip the wings of hand-raised budgerigars, never aviary bred budgerigars, as it can seem inhumane. Budgerigars kept inside may suffer from molting issues. Budgerigars molt based on seasonal changes in the environment. In a controlled area (like an air conditioned room) the bird doesn't experience seasonal fluctuations, which can cause molting irregularities. Molting tonics are available and should be given every month for budgerigars kept inside.

Bathing your bird
Birds need to bathe every day so that their skin and feathers stay healthy, but never use any type of soap or detergent, as this will strip

the feathers of essential oils. For small birds, provide a bird bath in the cage – one or two inches of water will be enough, and the bird will bathe itself. For larger birds, spray with lukewarm water from a mister, or let the bird bath in the kitchen sink.

Budgerigars might defecate a lot but they also like to stay clean. They even like to go under water for fun. Look at your favorite pet shop for a stable mini-bathtub made out of plastic that you can hook to the cage. It must be accessible for the budgerigar and easy to refill from the outside.

- Don't fill the bath too much. You don't want the budgerigar to spill water on the bottom of the cage every time he goes in the bathtub.
- The bathtub must be roughly the size of the bird so he can immerse himself in the water.
- A bathtub is great for your pet budgerigar and they are sure to love it but make sure it doesn't take up a lot of room in the cage. Budgerigars will clean themselves if you spray some water on them; it's not a must for them to have a bird bath.

Clean out the budgerigar's cage at least once a week
This will keep the budgerigar safe from diseases and germs. Clean only with mild dish soap and water and avoid using any cleaning products unless you are one hundred percent sure that they are safe for birds.

Create a good environment for your budgerigar to sleep
When it's time to sleep, simply throw a light towel or blanket over the cage. Make sure there is sufficient air ventilation - you don't want to suffocate your new bird! Make sure that the bird cannot get its nails caught in the fabric.

This is also helpful when it's noisy. The blanket will muffle most sounds, and will also keep cold drafts out. If your budgerigar is frightened by the dark, add a little night-light. Don't let your bird panic. It might fly around the cage and injure itself.

Tracking a budgarigar

If you keep your budgerigar outside it is recommended that you find a way to track your bird in case it escapes. There are various methods to achieve this, namely investing in a neck band or leg band.

Chapter 7. Budgerigar Nutrition

The knowledge of bird nutrition is constantly evolving. This is due to heightened awareness of the importance of nutrition and to increased research into birds' different needs. As with all other animals, birds need a proper balance of carbohydrates, proteins, fat, vitamins, minerals and water. Different species of birds often require different foods.

It is important to continually strive to improve your bird's diet, as a poor diet is often linked to several health problems. This involves constantly educating yourself as well as a certain degree of common sense. It is not sufficient to feed a budgerigar just to maintain life; instead, your goal should be to help it thrive and flourish. Your bird's health depends on how well it is fed.

What should I feed my budgerigar?

1. Seeds
Wild budgerigars would eat a great variety of seed types in the wild as different plants come into season. Commercial seed mixes may contain from 2 - 8 different kinds of seeds. However, they tend to be high in fat and carbohydrates and provide a decreased or imbalanced source of many nutrients if fed as the only source of food, which could lead to ill health and potentially shorten the life of your budgerigar. The problem is that a budgerigar will selectively eat only 1 or 2 of its favorite types of seed. Millet seed is often chosen preferentially. Owners will often also offer a millet spray or branch. This, of course, is more of the same seed and leads to further malnutrition. Honey sticks are often also offered, but once again, these contain more seeds that are stuck together with sugar and honey. Molting foods, song foods and conditioning foods are also available. These products are simply different combinations of more seeds that really have no particular bearing on the condition that they

claim to treat. Healthy molts, vibrant song and strong condition are achieved with a balanced diet all of the time.

Seeds are highly palatable and preferentially sought after, but nutritionally they are like giving candy to a child every day. Seeds should only be a small part of a balanced diet but should never be the entire diet. If you gradually offer your bird fewer seeds, your bird will start eating more of other properly balanced diets.

How much seed should I offer?
As a guideline, most budgerigars can be maintained on 1.5 - 2 level-measure teaspoons of seeds per bird, per day in a shallow dish, depending on the size of the bird. If there is more than one budgerigar in the cage, separate dishes should be used for each bird to ensure those birds at the bottom of the pecking order have a chance to eat. This may not be possible in a flock situation. If there are any seeds left over in the dish at the end of the day, it suggests that too many seeds were offered originally.

2. Pelleted Diets
Mature budgerigars are particularly troublesome to convert to a pelleted diet. Pellets have been developed to meet all your bird's nutritional needs. Different formulations are available for different life stages and for the management of certain diseases. Hand-raised babies are the easiest to start on a pelleted diet. Pellets are the ideal diet, therefore you are encouraged to slowly wean seed-eating birds onto a pelleted diet. Pellets should ideally represent approximately 75-80% of the bird's diet. There are many good brands of pelleted foods on the market place and pellets come in different flavors, colors and shapes.

How do I convert my bird to a pelleted diet?
Converting seed eating birds (seed-aholics) onto a pelleted diet is not always easy. Initially, pellets are not likely even identified as food. Slowly wean the bird off seeds over a period of 4-8 weeks while

having pellets constantly available in a separate dish. Some people mix the pellets in a reduced amount of seed to aid its acceptance in the cage, but you should be aware that the bird will not accidentally eat a pellet. It may take days, weeks or months to modify a bird's diet. Never withdraw seeds entirely without first being certain the bird is eating the pellets plus some fruits and vegetables. Birds are stubborn but can be trained.

Remember that you train the bird; do not let it train you. Consult your veterinarian if encountering any problems with this transition or with the health of your bird.

3. Fruits and Vegetables

Fruits, vegetables and greens should account for approximately 20 - 25% of the daily diet. Pale vegetables, with a high water composition (i.e. Iceberg, Head lettuce, celery) offer very little nutritional value. Avocado is reported to be potentially toxic.

Fruits and vegetables must be washed thoroughly to remove chemicals. Cut them into manageable pieces depending on the size of the bird. It is not necessary to take the skin off. Offer fruits and vegetables in a separate dish. If your bird appears to develop a particular fancy for one food item, reduce its volume or stop feeding it temporarily to promote the eating of other foods.

For optimal health, organic vegetables should be offered daily. Vegetables are best fed raw. For the biggest nutritional punch, focus mostly on dark green leafy vegetables (some favorites are dandelion leaves, parsley, cilantro, kale, spinach) and orange veggies (carrots, sweet potatoes, yams, pumpkin). Herbs and spices are excellent as well – keep reading for details.

Some suggested food items include: apple cherries (not the pit), peaches, apricots, Chinese vegetables (bok choy), pear asparagus, coconut, peas, banana, corn peppers (red/green), beans (cooked), cucumber, pineapple, chickpeas, dates, plum, kidney, dandelion leaves, pomegranate, lentils, dates, potato, endive, pumpkin, mung fig, rappini, navy grapes, raspberry, soy, grapefruit, rice (brown), beet, kale, romaine lettuce, blueberry, kiwi, spinach, broccoli, melons, sprouted seeds, Brussel sprouts, mango, squash, cabbage, nectarines, strawberry, cantaloupe, orange, sweet potato, carrot, papaya, tomato, parsnip, zucchini.

A well-balanced diet must be maintained at all times.

4. Water

Fresh, clean water must be available at all times. Depending on the quality of your tap water, you might consider the use of bottled water. Dishes must be cleaned thoroughly every day with soap and water.

Daily Feeding Routine

Breakfast: 1-2 teaspoons (per budgerigar) of an organic, sprouted mix of seeds, grains, and legumes. (Note: I provide the ingredients and directions below so you can make your own). Add 1 tablespoon of chopped, organic vegetables and/or fruit.

Afternoon Meal: Throw away breakfast meal remains and wash the food dish with soap and hot water. This meal is identical to the breakfast meal however it is important to offer a fresh batch to avoid spoilage or bacterial infection.

Bedtime: An hour before you tuck your budgerigar(s) in for the night, remove the afternoon meal remains and wash the dish. Provide 1 scant teaspoon (per budgerigar) of a dry seed or pellet mix for late night munching. Avoid products that contain color dyes, artificial flavors, chemical preservatives, and other additives. Try Kaylor of Colorado, Harrison's, or Dr. Harvey's. Remember to limit processed convenience foods to 20% of your parakeet's total diet.

Note: Parakeets hull their seeds, which means they take the "skin" off the outside of the seed before eating it. This "skin" normally drops back into the dish, so it may look like their dish is full. Don't be fooled by a dish of empty seed hulls!

Keep in the cage at all times:
- 1 teaspoonful of herbs and spices (see ingredients on this page below to make your own)
- Cuttlebone
- Mineral block
- Clean water

Treats:
The favorite treats to use during handling and training is organic hulled millet. Using hulled seeds means there's no shell mess to clean up afterward.

Sprouting Instructions
1.   Ingredients: Below, I provide a list of suitable ingredients so you can make your own sprouting mix.
2.   Clean: Place 4 days worth of an organic sprouting mix into a small stainless steel fine mesh strainer. Rinse the mix with cool water until the water runs clear. (Note: 1 budgerigar fed twice daily will typically consume about 8 teaspoons in 4 days.)
3.   Soak: Spoon the mix into a clean glass container. Cover the mix with cool water. Soak the mix for 8-10 hours at room temperature.
4.   Rinse and drain: After soaking for 8-10 hours, pour the soaked mix into a clean, small stainless steel fine mesh strainer. Using cold water, rinse the mix in the strainer until the water runs clear. Drain thoroughly.
5.   Sprout: Place the strainer over a bowl to catch water drips. Keep the strainer at room temperature (70° is optimal), away from direct sunlight, and where air circulates (not in a cupboard). While

sprouting, make sure to thoroughly rinse and drain the mix in the strainer at least twice daily. Let the sprouting progress for at least 8 hours and up to 4 days. Long sprout tails are not necessary, in fact, most birds prefer to eat them while the sprout tails or roots are just barely visible.

6.   Apple cider vinegar and serve: Adding a short apple cider vinegar soak right before serving is beneficial, as it helps to guard against bacteria and fungi. Buy your apple cider vinegar from the natural food store — it should be organic, raw, and unfiltered. "Bragg" is a good brand. Right before serving each meal portion, rinse the sprouts in a strainer, then soak one meal portion of the sprouts in 1/2 cup water containing 1/2 teaspoon of organic apple cider vinegar for 10 minutes. Drain well and serve the food immediately.

7.   Cleanliness and freshness: To avoid toxic bacterial infections, remove old food and replace with a fresh batch at least every 8 hours (feed twice daily). If you live in a hot or humid climate without air conditioning, you may need to remove the remains as soon as 1-2 hours. Scrub all feeding and sprouting utensils, strainers, dishes and jars with hot, soapy water after each use. I keep twice as many feeding dishes as I have cages so that I can run the used ones through the dishwasher for easy sterilization. If your cage doesn't have a bottom grill, remove and replace the newspapers on the bottom of the cage every day so that your birds won't have access to old, rotting food that has fallen from their food bowl.

8.   Refrigerate: I feed the sprouted mix straight from the strainer, at room temperature, within 4 days. However, if you still have some leftovers after sprouting for 4 days, then thoroughly rinse, drain, and refrigerate the leftovers. Smell the sprouts before feeding — if it smells musty or sour, toss it out and start a new batch.

Organic sprouting parakeet food

You don't need to buy every ingredient listed below all at once. Instead, provide a variety over time. Mix a few types of ingredients from each subcategory. For example, buy 2+ herb seeds, 2+ grains, 2+ oil seeds, and 2+ legumes. The diversity and balance of seeds, grains and legumes are complementary so that by feeding a variety, the blend alone is capable of providing the nutrients parrots require.

The weighted ratio I typically aim for in the total mix is roughly 50-60% grains, 20-25% legumes (peas, beans, and lentils), 8-12% herb seeds, and 8-12% oil seeds.

Buy seeds for sprouting from reputable sources. To take a standard mass-produced bird seed mix and attempt to sprout it may be asking for trouble. I use only human-grade, organic, vacuum-bagged seeds, legumes and grains that I buy from a natural health food grocer.

Note: All sprouting ingredients need to be raw and whole or "hulless" (not hulled). Do not use canned or roasted ingredients.

What about people food?

As a rule, any wholesome, nutritious food that you and your family eat your bird can eat. Follow the general guidelines discussed above and use your common sense. Some birds even enjoy a small amount of lean cooked meat, fish, egg or cheese occasionally. Dairy products should be consumed in moderation. It is common sense that junk food, chocolate, products containing caffeine and alcoholic beverages be avoided.

Will my bird have any different needs throughout its life?

Birds that are extremely young, stressed, injured, laying eggs or raising young may have certain special nutritional requirements. There are specially formulated pelleted foods available for birds with specific nutritional requirements. Consult your veterinarian regarding these situations.

Does my bird need extra vitamins, minerals or amino acids?

Your veterinarian can help you assess your bird's diet and its particular needs. One opinion suggests that a bird eating 75 - 80% of its diet in the form of pelleted food may not need supplements. Specific vitamins or minerals may be more important at various times during a bird's life (e.g. egg laying requires calcium supplementation). Calcium supplements are available if your budgerigar is determined to be deficient.

Powdered supplements are often regarded as more stable. Mix these supplements in water or preferably apply directly onto moist food. Placing these powders on seeds or dried foods is of little value since it will ultimately end up on the bottom of the food dish and not in the bird.

Does my bird need gravel or grit?

Controversy exists over the need for gravel. It was believed that grit was necessary for the mechanical breakdown of food in the gizzard, as an aid to digestion. However, now we know that birds do fine without grit in their diet. Some birds will in fact have problems if grit is over eaten.

Foods to avoid

Creating a list of foods considered dangerous or toxic to pet birds can be a challenge for many reasons. Just as people don't have the same reactions to certain foods that another person might have, a food that makes one species of bird ill doesn't necessarily cause illness in another species of bird. Birds belong to Class Aves, a large, diverse group in which there are many differences in anatomy and physiology; so different bird species will demonstrate different sensitivities to toxins.

Another consideration is that many incidents of pet birds having an adverse reaction to foods are based on bird owners' own accounts, which may not have been verified. For example, if a pet bird dies shortly after eating, the owner might jump to the conclusion that a particular food item killed his or her pet.

Pinpointing exactly how toxic a particular food is can also be tricky. A food can be eaten in small amounts or in moderation without problems, yet this same food item can cause illness or even death in birds if consumed in excessive amounts. An important consideration is that some of the toxicology information used by avian veterinarians has been directly transferred over from dog, cat and even human pediatric medicine; the assumption being that if the food is toxic to people and other pets, it may be toxic to birds as well.

Avian veterinarians rely on such a wide range of information, however, because it is generally considered best to err on the side of caution. Here is a breakdown of foods that are potentially toxic to pet birds, with accompanying degrees of caution.

- **Avocado:** All parts of the avocado plant contain persin, a fungicidal toxin that has been reported to be a cardiac toxin to birds. Small birds like canaries and budgerigars are considered to be more susceptible; however, clinical signs have been observed in other bird species. Clinical signs of respiratory distress usually develop 12 hours after ingestion and death can occur within one to two days.
- **Onion and garlic:** Onion and garlic toxicity is well recognized in dogs and cats. Those in concentrated forms, such as garlic powder or onion soup mix, are more potent than the raw vegetable form. Fatal toxicity has been described in geese fed large amounts of green onions, as well as a conure fed large amounts of garlic.
- **Comfrey:** This green leaf herb is popular with some canary breeders, but studies in human medicine have shown it can cause liver damage.
- **Fruit pits and apple seeds:** While diced apple is ok for pet birds, the apple seeds contain cyanide and should always be

51

removed prior to feeding apple to your bird. Pits from cherries, plums, apricots and peaches also contain cyanide so never allow your bird to chew on them.

- **High-fat, high-sodium, high-sugar foods:** Although not technically toxic, table foods laden with high concentrations of fat, salt and sugar can cause serious health problems in birds. Instead of offering your bird a bit of pasta with sauce, let it enjoy a noodle before you add the sauce, salt or butter.

- **Sugar-free candy:** Sugar-free candy might offer a better alternative to regular sweets for people, but it often contains the sugar alternative, xylitol, which has been associated with severe hypoglycemia and liver damage in dogs.

- **Spoiled or Soiled Food**: Remove all uneaten food and replace with a fresh batch at least twice daily to avoid deadly internal bacterial infections.

- **Supplements in their water**: Your bird should have fresh water every day. Don't add supplements unless your veterinarian tells you to; they can be a medium for bacteria to grow and can cause a bird to turn up his nose at his water bowl, leading to decreased water intake and kidney damage.

- **Any food that has been in your mouth**: Human saliva contains many toxic and bacterial substances that can be deadly to your bird.

- **Mushrooms**: Mushrooms are a fungus and some species are toxic.

- **Raw meat and poultry**: May carry salmonella and other bacteria.

- **Milk or raw milk (nonpasteurized) cheese**: Parrots can not digest dairy products containing lactose (the type of sugar contained in milk). Parrots are not mammals and so are not fed milk as babies — they feed their young by regurgitating food to them. Yogurts or low-fat cheese in very small amounts are okay because their initial lactose has been transformed.

- **Potatoes**: Potatoes are not toxic in themselves, but certain parts of them are: the skin as well as the green parts you sometimes see on their flesh. These green bits contain solanine, a toxic alkaloid that forms when potatoes are overexposed to light. This alkaloid can affect the central nervous system if ingested in significant quantity. It also is necessary to remove the germinated parts and potato eyes, since these also contain solanine.
- **Eggplant**: Another member of the Solanaceae family (with the potato), eggplants contain toxic solanine.
- **Green tomatoes**: They contain tomatine, a substance like solanine. The plants and the leaves of green tomatoes are toxic.
- **Honey**: Can contain a toxic bacterium that produces the neurotoxin botulin: clostridium botulinum.
- **Chocolate**: It's toxic to many animals, birds included.
- **Junk food, alcohol, caffeine, tobacco**: Duh, right?

Toxic items

Never let your budgerigar play with or touch an item unless you know it is safe and non-toxic. Any metallic objects containing heavy metals, such as lead, zinc, copper, or brass, are poisonous to birds and can poison them simply through contact with the beak or skin. Safe metals include stainless steel, iron, and ungalvanized tin. For more information, see "Heavy Metal Poisoning in Birds" by Gillian Willis. You also need to be very careful with items which have paint or glue. You need to be sure that any paint or glue in or on an item is non-toxic. If you don't know what an item is made of, it is better to be safe than sorry by not letting your budgerigar play with it.

Toxic plants

Some plants and parts of plants are poisonous to birds, so you need to research any plant that you have in the house or that you use to make perches to be sure it is safe. If you can't identify it or can't determine whether if it is safe, then it is better to be safe than sorry by not letting your budgerigar come into contact with it. Furthermore, when procuring branches to use as perches, you must disinfect them properly. Wipe the branches with a diluted bleach solution (3/4 cup bleach per 1 gallon of water) and then bake in the oven at 200° F (90° C) until they are dry (this disinfection routine should be done by an adult). Aerosol sprays are dangerous to birds.

Household cleaners and chemicals
You should never let your budgerigar come into contact with household cleaners or chemicals. Additionally, birds have very sensitive respiratory systems, and you must avoid using aerosol or sprayed products (including cleaners, fragrances, deodorizers, and beauty products) around your budgerigars, as well as cleaners with strong chemical smells or fragrances. You should also not use any kind of fragrance products, such as candles, plug-ins, sprays, and potpourri if you have a budgerigar in the house. When it comes time for you to use a cleaner or chemical in your home, put your budgerigar's cage into a room the fumes will not get into, or if it's a nice day place the cage outside out of direct sunlight. Your budgerigar will need to stay out for at least a few hours and until all the fumes or smells are gone.

Another source of toxic fumes in the home is a non-stick coating (PTFE), which comes under many names, including Teflon©. When non-stick coating is overheated, it releases toxic fumes which kill birds very quickly. Even under normal heating conditions, non-stick coating can release some toxic fumes. It is recommended that you never use cookware or appliances with non-stick coating when you have birds in the home.

How to encourage your budgerigar to eat new foods
The key to optimum parakeet nutrition is variety, however, if your parakeet has eaten little except pre-packaged, mass-produced dry seed before, it will need time to get used to different foods.

Sometimes the transition to a new, better diet takes many weeks, but don't give up — keep their long term nutritional health in mind. Don't change foods suddenly; do so gradually and make certain that he is eating the new food before removing all of the old. Here are some tips on encouraging your budgerigar to eat new foods:

- For the first week or two, sprinkle this favorite seeds on top of the new food. After this initial introduction, mix a small amount of the seeds into the new food to encourage exploration.
- Offer the new food items as an appetizer — before breakfast when it is most hungry.
- Many budgerigars will be encouraged to try new foods by peer pressure — observing another bird eating the food. Lacking another bird, try placing the new food on a mirror. If your bird is bonded with you, be his role model.
- Try moistening leafy green vegetables before offering as budgerigars often like to bathe on them, and then eat them.
- Try serving large chunks of veggies for them to chew pieces off, as well as finely grated and mixed into their sprouts.
- If after several weeks your budgerigar continues to pick out his favorite ingredients and leaves the rest, try coarsely grinding a mixture of his normal food with the new food items (right before serving) to make it difficult for him to be picky. A coffee bean or spice grinder works well for small batches; a food processor for large batches. You will need to remove uneaten, ground-up foods from the cage within 30-60 minutes (depending on your climate) because it will spoil much faster than whole foods and sprouts will.

Chapter 8. Breeding Your Budgerigars

Budgerigar breeding may sound like a great hobby and it is! However, you need lots of knowledge. You also need to make all of the budgerigars happy and healthy to make a happy family. Breeding budgerigars takes time and isn't easy. You need to cash out on supplies and feed, check on the budgerigars often, clean the cage daily and set aside extra time for caring for the chicks. The room should be quiet, protected from predators including pets, have no disturbances and the only person entering the room should be you.

Selecting a Pair

- Both the male and female you wish to breed should be at least one year old.
- Selecting a pair that is already bonded will help ensure a shorter time until they begin to mate and lay eggs.
- If you wish to breed for a certain variety, learn about budgerigar varieties and genetics.

Set-up

- Each pair should be set up in their own cage at least 24"w x 16"d x 16"h (70x40x40cm). The cage should not have a grate on the bottom. If the cage has an permanent grate, place the newspaper lining on top of the grate. Use only black and white newspaper to line the bottom.
- A wooden nest box should be attached outside of the breeding cage.
- A wooden insert with a concave circle should be at the bottom of the nesting box to prevent splayed legs.
- Pine shavings (unscented) should be layered in the bottom of the box over the wooden insert. The hen will adjust the pine shavings to her liking.
- It is very important to have a cuttlebone and mineral block in the cage. An iodine salt spool is also recommended.

56

- At least two perches should be provided. Try to provide variety in perches, including a safe, natural wood branch.
- Food and water dishes should be provided. I recommend attaching two water tubes, especially after all the babies have hatched. I also recommend putting a large jar feeder on the cage floor. The parents will go through a lot of seed and water when caring for a nest full of growing chicks.
- Pieces of soft wood for the female budgerigar to chew on will satisfy her need for gnawing and also can help get her into the mood to breed. Be sure the wood is safe for birds by buying this material at a bird or pet store.
- If only breeding one or a couple of pairs, you will need a large cage to put the babies into when they are weaned. If breeding large scale, you will need to build a flight cage to keep non-breeding budgerigars and newly weaned babies in.

Environment and timing

It is better to start out with 2 or 3 pairs because they help stimulate each other into the breeding mode. In addition, if something goes wrong with a pair, you would be able to foster out the chicks under another pair. In the US, the best results for breeding season is from October through March. The most comfortable temperatures to keep them in is 65 to 75 degrees Fahrenheit (18 to 24 degrees Celsius). Some humidity helps the eggs to hatch better.

They need good light, but not direct sun during the day. They need 12 hours of darkness with the cage covered at night. Try to go by the sun; cover the budgerigars at sundown and uncover them around 6 to 7AM each morning. It is important to use a full-spectrum light bulb in the breeding room to assist in the vitamin-D formation and to allow for proper vision.

Budgerigars need to have a comfortable environment and to be healthy and happy to breed.

Proper care of breeding pairs

Budgerigars need a very good diet when breeding, including vitamin supplements. Organic, fresh greens should be provided daily. Examples are dandelion leaves or carrot-tops. All produce must be organic! Even a tiny amount of pesticides are enough to kill a baby chick. Bits of shredded carrots are good too. In addition, give them little bits of cooked chicken or egg for protein, but only when breeding. The better variety of good foods you feed, the healthier the chicks will be.

Try not to interfere too much with the breeding birds. Have a regular routine when you clean the cage. Keep the breeding cages very clean. Change the food and water each day. Check the food and water levels both in the morning and night.

Nest boxes should be checked once per day, preferably when the hen comes out to poop and stretch her wings. Remove broken egg shells or any dead chicks right away.

Budgerigar pairs will try to have a third clutch, right after the first two, in one breeding season. However, if they have successfully reared chicks from the previous two clutches, they should be stopped from starting the third clutch for health reasons, to prevent burnout, weak chicks, etc. Furthermore, the pair should be rested for a whole year until the next breeding season. To stop a pair, remove the mother from the cage when the youngest chick is about 10 days old. The father will take over the care of the chicks. Watch them closely for the first 48 hours, as it sometimes takes a day or so for dad to realize that mom isn't coming back and he needs to take over. If you notice the babies' crops empty, you may need to give a hand feeding.

Proper care of the chicks

If you need to handle the eggs, be sure to completely clean your hands with soap and water before handling. Bacteria from your hands can be absorbed through the shell, which can harm the baby.

When the youngest chick hatches, the oldest chick will be much bigger than it, especially with large clutches of more than 5 eggs. When you check the nest box, make sure the youngest chicks are not getting trampled and are getting fed (you will see food in their crops). If you notice any problems, you can try fostering the youngest chicks to another pair with similarly aged chicks. You may also try fostering newly hatched chicks to a pair with eggs. Most of the time a fostered chick is accepted. Check often on a fostered chick to make sure. If you see food in the baby's crop, the pair has accepted him.

When the babies start getting feathered, it will be about time to start cleaning the nest box. If you notice a large build-up of soiled shavings and the babies tend to be getting a lot of droppings stuck to their feet, start changing the bedding about once a week, or as needed. Remove the babies into a large bowl lined with a towel and scoop out the soiled bedding.

Scrape the wood insert as needed and replace with fresh bedding. You may need to block the entrance to the nest box while you do this to prevent the hen from coming into the box. Check the babies every day for fixable developmental problems. Check under the top mandible (beak) for buildup of food, which can cause an undershot beak. If you notice food stuck under the top mandible, remove gently and carefully with a toothpick.

Make sure the chick isn't developing splayed legs. If this is happening, try adding extra pine shavings. If a young baby develops splayed legs, the problem can be corrected because their bones are still forming. You will have to tie the legs close together to facilitate proper development. See the article Splayed Legs by Wanda Barras for more detailed information.

When the chicks start coming out of the nest, provide a shallow dish of food on the bottom of the cage to facilitate weaning. You can remove a 6 week old weaned chick from its parents in the breeding cage. It should be put in a large cage reserved for young birds or in the flight cage. Provide lots of food, available in different places, especially in a dish on the bottom of the cage. Keep a close eye on newly removed chicks to make sure they are eating. Check their crops to make sure they are full before covering their cage at night.

Development and what to expect
When the hen starts to lay eggs, she will lay an egg every other day. A clutch of eggs is normally anywhere from 4 to 6 eggs, but sometimes 8 or more.

A new hen may not start to brood the eggs until the second or even third egg is laid. This is fine and will not harm the eggs' viability. It takes 17 to 20 days for the eggs to hatch.

You can watch the babies develop within the egg! Purchase a very small flashlight such as the Maglite Solitaire. In a darkened room, shine the flashlight into one end of the egg. In a fertilized egg, you can see the embryo develop. It is the small red kidney shaped thing attached to the wall of the egg among the blood vessels. You can even see its heart beating if you look closely.

Looking after budgerigar chicks
Even whilst sitting on her eggs, keep an eye on your female. If the cere turns blue on your hen, you need to act immediately, as this means she is losing condition and will struggle to feed the chicks. Being unwell can cause your hen to become violent, and it is not unheard of for chicks to die or be featherless at the hands of their distressed mother. During this period, the male will feed the hen,

who in turn feeds the chicks. Therefore, it is imperative that both your cock and hen are well cared for.

Once hatched, check subtly and regularly. It is the only way you can check if they are being fed, and that siblings aren't smothering each other. Don't be worried if you have chicks of all shapes and sizes. The chicks will hatch at different times, sometimes days apart, and therefore their development will vary. If your hen has an unmanageable number of chicks, you can foster them to other pairs that are breeding.

Between 10 and 15 days after hatching, the feathers will start to come through on the chicks. At this point, you can change the bedding in the nest box and check their limb development. Calmly close off the entrance to the nesting box so that the hen cannot enter. She will be quite happy in the cage with the male but do not keep the chicks away from the mother for too long.

Gently scoop the chicks out of the nest box and place them in a bowl lined with a soft towel. You can then check each chick individually and get them used to being handled. At around 20 days old, the chicks will start to move out of the nest. At this point, provide them with extra food to encourage weaning and a shallow bowl at the bottom of the cage for foraging. With so many small additions to the cage, it is best to insert another water bottle. Now that the chicks are out and about, handle them as regularly as you can, and teach them to perch on shoulders and fingers!

When the chicks are six weeks old, they will need to be moved to another cage. They will be fully feathered at this age and ready to learn to fly. Moving them to a large cage will allow them to harness this skill. Having a cage with different heights of perch will help the chicks gain strength and become experts in the air. At this point you can either let the chicks go to new forever homes or move them into a large aviary with all the older birds; some of which may be relatives.

Clean the nesting box and cage frequently
Chicks also mean poop, so the nest box must be cleaned out regularly. When the hen is out eating, remove the chicks to a small container lined with soft paper towels. Scrape out the soiled bedding and scrape away wet poops from the bottom of the nest box, and then replace the nesting materials with fresh stuff. Gently replace chicks back. Make sure to be as quick as possible. (This should not be done until all fertile eggs have hatched.

Chapter 9. Budgerigar Health

Budgerigars, like all birds, are very adept at concealing their illness. This is a self-preservation mechanism, as the sick and the weak are the ones predators will focus on. By the time your pet looks ill, you can assume that your pet is seriously sick and is likely to deteriorate quickly unless appropriate treatment is provided.

By observing your pet daily you will learn its normal behavior and you will be able to notice anything out of the ordinary. Below is a list of things to look out for as possible indicators of disease/illness; and a vet may need to be consulted.

Signs of a healthy budgerigar
• Feathers: clean, smooth and nice bright, crisp markings.
• Posture: upright, natural and alert.
• Beak, cere, eyes and feet: all clear and without any discharge or extra roughness or growths.
• Vent: clear, without any build up of droppings.
• Breathing: smooth and regular, not faster than usual or labored (panting), not noisy.

All these things indicate a healthy, happy bird. The other factor is the behavior of your budgerigar. It may alter its behavior, become quieter or agitated, sleep more, for example, before any physical symptoms show, so it is also important that you know your birds' normal routine and behavior.

Remember, budgerigars are a prey animal and one of the features that go along with this is pretending you are well, even if you are not. If they look sick they are probably worse than you think - get help earlier rather than later.

Symptoms of illness

At some time there is bound to be something that goes wrong with your bird's health. It is a good idea to have a first aid kit handy; it may save your pets life!

For each of the features below, I have given a brief description of what you should keep an eye out for.

- Feathers and skin: An ill budgerigar will often sit fluffed up more than normal. They may seem to be otherwise normal but a bit fluffier, this can be because they have a low temperature and are trying to stay warm. As they get worse they will become less active and appear to be sleeping a lot. If your budgerigar becomes very unwell it may sit fluffed up with its eyes shut like it is asleep but without its beak tucked under its wing.... try to get your bird help long before this stage. Any problems with the skin or feathers themselves could also be due to parasites.

- Posture: This ties in with the feathers a bit, being fluffed up and more hunched than usual. Sometimes the wings and/or tail will drop, making the budgerigar seem tired and weak. Again, this is a sign that things are seriously wrong.

- Beak, cere, eves and feet: There are a few things to watch for in these areas. The first is any discharge from the beak, nostrils and eyes. These may make the feathers around the face wet and mucky. Also watch for sneezing, coughing, etc. Regularly check this area for growths and roughness or any scaly looking bits. Issues here can be due to parasites or respiratory problems. Also check out the information on beak and toe nail trimming.

- Vent: The most obvious sign here is mucky feathers caused by diarrhea. In addition, any blood should be checked out immediately. Problems here can be due to digestive or reproductive problems.

- Breathing: Be sure you are used to how your budgerigar normally breathes. If it is panting, breathing faster than usual or even less than usual then it is a sign of problems. A budgerigar that is unwell will often have its tail bobbing in time with its breathing when it is having breathing difficulties.

If your budgerigar shows symptoms of illness it pays to get veterinary advice soon. If you can find an avian vet it is best, as many vets do not have much experience with small birds. However, if you can't then a vet that treats birds is the next best thing. Make sure you have found a vet before you need one! You do not want to be trying to find one while your pet suffers.

Common Ailments

Budgerigars are relatively robust creatures, but can still fall victim to a wide range of ailments. You should always rely on a veterinary expert to make the diagnosis. Your task as a budgerigar owner is to recognize illness in general terms, then seek a vet's opinion for diagnosis.

Lice

Feather lice look like tiny dark lines, about 2mm long, and lay along the feather barbules, especially on the underside of the wings. They are basically harmless, though unsightly if you know they are there. They want nothing to do with humans, as we have no feathers. They can be easily be treated with an anti-parasite treatment for birds that you can get at any pet store. I have found that a product called Mite and Lice Bird Spray is very effective at quickly eliminating feather lice.

Scaly face mites

Scaly face mites cause the buildup of scale growths to occur on the beak, on the legs, and/or around the eyes, where the skin is exposed. If left unchecked, the mite can cause deformations to the budgerigar's beak and face. The picture on the right is an example of an advanced, untreated case of the scaly face (this bird was found in

65

a poorly kept pet shop). Several treatments are available, the best of which is Ivomec or ivermectin. You can get this medicine in a product sold at bird stores, or from an avian veterinarian. You must follow the instructions provided by the vet or listed on the product carefully. If you want to try, you can treat this non-medically. You can use shortening (like Crisco) or vegetable oil. Rub a bit on the affected areas, twice a day for about a week. It is important to disinfect the cage and all accessories, once at the beginning and once at the end of treatment. These pests do not infest humans.

Red mites
Red mites are oval shaped and have a lighter mark on the back. The Red mite can be introduced to aviaries by wild birds in the vicinity. These minute parasites live in dark cracks in woodwork and similar sites, venturing out in darkness to feed on the budgerigar's blood. Birds which are breeding are at particular risk because they spend most of the day and night in the nest box. Both chicks and adult birds are at risk, and anemia will develop in severe cases.

Feather-plucking can result from the irritation caused by the mites. Their numbers can increase very rapidly in warm conditions, and they are capable of surviving in small numbers, without feeding, in cages or nest boxes from one breeding season to the next.
They can be detected by covering a cage with a white cloth at night and then examining the inner side of this the next morning for small red or black specks, which are the engorged mites.

They can be treated with an anti-parasite spray for birds, but the best treatment is probably Ivomec or ivermectin prescribed by an avian vet. If you have a problem with this parasite, you should consult an avian vet for advice on treatment and prevention.

Avian Gastric Yeast (AGY) infection
Also known as macrorhabdiosis, or mega bacteriosis, this highly contagious infection is frustratingly difficult to spot in the early

stages. AGY incubates and proliferates in the bird with no outward sign of trouble. The first thing you might notice is that your budgerigar loses weight, in spite of eating with his usual gusto. This is because AGY impedes digestion. You may then spot undigested food in his droppings, or the bird may vomit food and mucus. He will also become listless.

Until 2004 the cause of the disease was thought to be bacteria, but it has now been identified as yeast, Latin name Macrorhabdus ornithogaster. The misdiagnosis came about due to bacteria, including Streptococcus, taking advantage of the budgerigar's hammered immune system and spreading secondary infection. The combination of the yeast and bacteria attack leads to a condition called wasting disease (sometimes called "going light").

Your vet will be able to administer a drug to combat the AGY and will recommend a healthy diet to aid recovery. This usually involves omitting all yeast-feeding sugary foodstuffs.

You will still need to keep a close eye on your birds, as AGY has the horrible habit of lying fallow and then blooming again a few weeks later.

Budgerigar Candidiasis
This is another yeast infection. Candida, the organism responsible, is a form of thrush (the virus, not the bird!), and can bloom anywhere in a budgerigar's digestive system from the crop downwards. Some of the symptoms are similar to AGY infection – listlessness, vomiting and loose droppings. The vomit will have a nasty smell, and the bird's crop may swell up, due to gases produced by the Candida yeast. In advanced cases, the budgerigar will suffer loss of balance and shaking fits.

Candidiasis can only be cured with drugs that kill the bacteria, so a trip to the vet is essential. The cure takes about one week, during which the budgerigar's diet should be closely controlled to avoid the ingestion of yeast-feeding sugars.

Budgerigar Sour Crop
This condition has more than one cause, but all the suspects are members of the yeast family. The symptoms are a swollen crop and sour-smelling vomit. Once again, it will take a targeted drug to kill the infection.

Parrot Fever (Psittacosis)
This is the bird-borne disease most people have heard of, due to it being transmittable to humans. Chlamydophia psittaci is the organism responsible for the condition, and it is estimated that 1% of wild birds harbor the disease, a figure that rises to 30% in captive budgerigars. Most of these are carriers, showing no symptoms themselves, but passing the disease on via their droppings and saliva. Keeping cages clean is therefore the best way of preventing the disease from spreading.

A bird that succumbs to parrot fever will display listlessness, ruffled feathers, breathing problems, loose green droppings, gummed up cere, etc.

The ill bird will need to visit a vet to verify his condition. Isolation is then vital, and the cage the bird came from will have to be disinfected. Monitor your other birds for symptoms, and remove any that you think may have succumbed. The vet will prescribe drugs, or may recommend that it is in everyone's best interest to have the bird humanely killed.

Fledgling Disease
Also known as Papovavirus, this is caused by the Psittacine polyomavirus virus, which kills the young birds before fledging. It does not affect adult birds, although there is the possibility that they

may be carriers of the virus. In a milder form, the virus produces a condition known as French molt (see below).

Wounds

Any wound on a bird can become infected and lead to septicemia (blood poisoning). This will finish off a small bird like a budgerigar very quickly. If you see any traces of blood on the birds or in the cage, make a visual examination to spot the wounded party. It could be a case of feather bleeding (see above), but is more likely to be an injury. Any flesh wound should be referred to a vet for antibiotic treatment.

Prevention is the best cure for this problem. Make sure the cage is free of sharp or pointed objects that could lead to wounds.

Splayed Feet

This is a condition that affects chicks that have been squatting on a flat nesting box floor while their leg bones develop. Setting up your nest box correctly should prevent the problem from occurring. If the legs are splayed, the condition can be remedied by taping the legs together between the ankle and the knee for a few days, with enough slack for the bird to move around. Consult an expert before attempting to do this, though.

Worms

Budgerigars can become infected with Ascaris roundworm. These creatures live and breed in animals' guts, and their eggs are passed on via droppings. The adult worms can grow 3.5cm long, which in a bird as small as a budgerigar is a major problem. Several of these in a budgerigar's gut can leach all the nutrients from the birds' food, causing severe malnutrition. In extreme cases, there can be paralysis, but more often the symptoms will be weight loss and listlessness.

A vet will prescribe a medicine that flushes the worms from the budgerigar's system. If successful, you will spot the adult creatures in the bird's droppings. Treatment will need repeating a few weeks later to catch the worms that survived as larvae in the budgerigar's gut. Ringworm is a particular problem in outdoor aviaries, where droppings fall to the earth – a perfect habitat for the worm eggs.

Air Sac Mites

Budgerigars, along with many other birds, have an internal organ called an air sac, part of their respiratory system. This is sometimes invaded by a tiny creature called the air sac mite. It also colonizes the bird's trachea (the breathing pipe between the throat and the lungs). An infestation will affect the budgerigar's voice. He will stop chirruping, his whistles will sound hoarse, and he will start to make a clicking, wheezing sound when he breathes. If left untreated the bird will eventually suffocate.

A vet will be able to treat the ill bird, along with the rest of your flock – the air sac mite can spread very quickly, and you have to assume that all the birds are infected. This may not be obvious, as it can take several weeks before the wheezing kicks in.

Feather Problems

You will be able to spot feather-related ailments far more easily than bacterial or fungal ones. Any permanent untidiness in the budgerigar's coat, or feather-loss that results in bald patches, is a very visible sign of trouble.

Budgerigar feather cyst

Cysts occur when a feather fails to break through the skin. It will continue to grow beneath the surface, producing a lump on the budgerigar's skin. The primary wing feathers are the most commonly affected ones. Cysts won't disappear without surgical intervention.

Feathers falling out

Feather loss could be due to one of five things: molting, parasites, self-plucking, French molt virus, or Psittacine Beak and Feather Disease. These are all dealt with elsewhere in this guide.

Feather plucking

If a budgerigar starts plucking its own feathers, there's an underlying health problem. Unfortunately, it's not obvious which of the many possible ailments is to blame. It could be parasites, an allergy, low air humidity, lack of fresh air, stress, boredom, mating hormones, liver disease, cancer, bacterial or fungal infection, malnutrition, heavy metal poisoning, or simply a bad habit.

A trip to the vet's is necessary to see if the underlying problem can be diagnosed, and if it turns out to be an environmental problem rather than disease, there are a few things you can do to get to the bottom of the plucking mystery:

- Watch your budgerigar closely, and see if you can spot a pattern or trigger. Is he plucking when angry, bored or stressed? Is another bird or object involved in the incident that leads up to a bout of plucking? Does it happen after he's eaten? Is he fine when you're around – i.e. does he only pluck when he's lonely?
- Assess the light, air and humidity situation. Is the budgerigar getting a 50/50 balance of light and dark through the 24 hour day? Can you do something about his centrally-heated, moisture-free environment to dampen things down a bit? Does moving the cage to a different location help?
- Swap the budgerigar's toys around, if you don't do so already. Make another stick perch to give him something novel to perch and nibble on.
- Is the bird in need of a bath? A simple case of itchy, dry, grubby skin could be the issue. Like a reluctant male teenager, if he's not in the habit of bathing, he may not realize that he needs one. A wide-nuzzled spray (not a fine

mist one) will get him wet and washing. The shower should induce the budgerigar's natural preening instincts, rather than his plucking ones. Don't overdo it, though, if the dousing is making the budgerigar panic.

- Check your food offerings against the list of good foods given in this guide. Try some new ones, to see if you can plug a difficult-to-pinpoint nutritional gap.
- Do you often stroke the budgerigar on the back or belly? This can stimulate mating hormones in the birds, which sometimes inspire feather-plucking.

Sadly, diagnosis is not the same as cure. Many budgerigars keep on plucking when the original stimulation has been identified and removed. If all angles have been covered and the budgerigar still plucks itself, you'll have to resign yourself to a semi-bald bird. Some contrary individuals simply get into the habit, and nothing you do will persuade them to desist.

Budgerigars plucking each other

This is a variation on the plucking problem. A budgerigar that is plucked by his cage mates will become much stressed, and can even die as a result. Isolating the perpetrator is the best short-term solution, but you will also have to assess the problem and see if you can resolve it in the long-term. The guilty bird may have been frustrated – these issues are often sex-related. Providing a nest-box or a choice of potential mates may divert the bird's frustrations away from plucking. Making sure there is more than one feeding station might help, too.

Feather Bleeding

When a budgerigar is growing new feathers during the molting season, or when young birds are producing their adult plumage, feather bleeding can occur. A new 'pin' feather contains blood vessels, without which the full feather would not be able to grow. If these are damaged during the early days, they will bleed like any other wound.

A patch of blood on an adult bird's coat is most likely to be one of these pin feathers. In extreme situations, the damage can result in the loss of so much blood that the budgerigar can actually die. The larger pin feathers – those associated with primary wing and tail feathers – bleed the most if damaged.

Once spotted, the bleeding must be addressed at once. The budgerigar must be caught, and the broken end of the feather must be held tightly for ten minutes. (Note: the pressure should be exerted on the feather itself, not the bird's body – squeezing the budgerigar can cause suffocation.) Once the bleeding has stopped, arrange a trip to the vet to have the broken pin feather removed.

Pin feathers above the cere and nostrils can easily break, but the bleeding involved here is minimal and soon stops. Budgerigars often damage these pins in a violent 'kissing' bout. A lone budgerigar will often bash himself against his 'friend' in the cage mirror and damage the new feathers. Once the blood has dried, it will leave a small stain above the cere which may remain until the next molt.

Feather Duster
Feather Duster Syndrome is a genetic condition, often a sign of inbreeding. The unfortunate afflicted birds – sometimes called Mops – have feathers that grow in random directions, and keep on growing. This gives them a 'feather duster' or mop-like appearance. Sometimes the beak and toenails grow abnormally long too. The budgerigars cannot fly or walk, and there are no plus sides to this genetic defect – the unhappy bird is unable to fend for itself, and has a weak immune system, with so much of the body's energy going towards endless feather growth. Such a bird will need a fortified diet. Even so, most of them do not make it beyond one year, and euthanasia is the humane option.

French molt

French molt is a virus that affects some juvenile birds, a mild form of the fatal fledgling disease. It causes secondary wing feathers and tail feathers to fall out, rendering the budgerigar incapable of flight. In severe cases, feathers fall out across much of the bird's body. There is no surefire cure, but a trip to the vet for formal diagnosis and advice is recommended.

Beak and Feather Disease

Psittacine Beak and Feather Disease (PBFD), or Psittacine Circovirus Disease (PCD), is a virus that causes feathers to fall out and beaks and toenails to become misshapen. There is no single pattern to the symptoms, which can range from a bedraggled-looking bird to a completely naked one. Skin sores and blemishes may appear too. The virus is passed on through drippings, and there is no cure. This makes it vital that you isolate the affected birds, and get a proper diagnosis from a vet.

Conclusion

Many people know them as "parakeets," but their real name is budgerigar, and you can find them in almost any continent you travel to!

The little budgerigar bird is one of the most popular pets in the world, ranking just behind dogs and cats, and it's no wonder. This affectionate, cute bird is small and inexpensive, and if trained properly a budgerigar can mimic human speech. This little bird is a charming companion for most pet owners.

Budgerigars aren't all fun and games, though, so before you bring one home, make sure you're not in for any surprises. I hope that this book has helped you to prepare for these suprises and that you may use it as a guide whenever you find yourself in need of advice on caring for your beloved pet.

Thank you for buying this book.

Printed in Great Britain
by Amazon